Contents

Introduction and aims

National Curriculum History was introduced as a foundation subject in 1991, and has since been slimmed down and revised.

Desirable outcomes for the learning of pre-compulsory school age children were published in 1996, one of which included a focus on history teaching and learning. Schools are therefore expected to teach history in line with these two documents.

In recent years, standards have continued to improve in history, with pupils (in Key Stages 1 and 2) satisfactory or better in more than four-fifths of lessons and good or very good in a quarter. This is associated with increasing command of the subject matter.

Recent research suggests that the key to improving teaching and learning is staff who discuss their classroom organisation and activities (both formally and informally), and who are prepared to monitor and reflect on their practice. This book could form the basis for school discussions about effective history practice, either for an informal discussion of the suggested ideas or for a whole-staff discussion on monitoring standards.

The bottom line should be children and their progress. This handbook supports manageable, exciting and enjoyable history teaching that has some impact on the children and their progress. Good luck with that vital task.

Aims of the handbook

To support the teaching and learning of primary history by:

☞ considering the nature of history and what it means in the primary school

☞ ensuring that the National Curriculum is understood and can be translated into plans which result in progression and purposeful teaching

☞ offering examples of ways in which children can be encouraged to work as historical detectives

☞ supporting effective practice that results in the development of knowledge, skills and understanding

☞ supporting teachers in the task of auditing existing policy, plans and practice and in producing new documentation

☞ offering ways to ensure effective practice by evaluation and monitoring by teachers and children

☞ considering approaches for differentiation in the classroom

☞ suggesting ways to challenge and stimulate children with appropriate questioning strategies

☞ offering ideas for different approaches to recording work

☞ helping teachers to make the most of resources, giving advice for resource boxes and teacher support material.

A PRIMARY TEACHER'S HANDBOOK – *History*

A Primary Teacher's

...ook

...ry

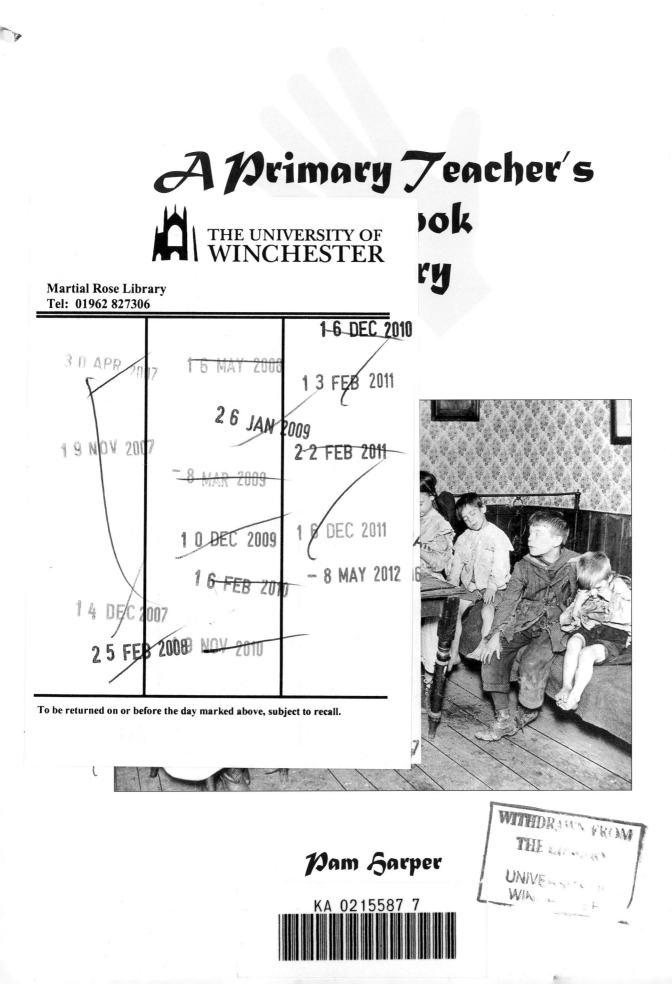

Pam Harper

Acknowledgements

The author and publisher would like to thank the following:
Clare House Primary School, Crofton Infant School, Crofton Junior School, Oaklands Junior School and Kelsey Park Nursery School, all in the London borough of Bromley, and Sarah, Jenny and Kate, three very special young historians.

Photographs:
Barnardo's, page 37
British Library, page 43
Francis MacKay, pages 35, 63
Justine Chadwick, pages 21, 22, 49, 50
Gary Cornford, pages 7, 26
Pam Harper, pages 4, 13, 23, 25, 34, 35, 38, 57
Steve Harrison, pages 1, 8, 12, 17, 24, 27, 40, 46, 47, 54, 55, 62
Michael Holford, page 42
Luton Museum, page 21
Manchester Public Libraries, page 41
Pete Ryan, pages 44, 45, 56, 64
Sara Le-Surf, page 41
York Archeological Trust, page 33

Reproductions:
Mr and Mrs George Byam and their eldest daughter, Selina, by Thomas Gainsborough, courtesy of Bridgeman Art Library, page 39
Plan of the town of Mexico, 16th century, reproduced letter by Hernan Cortès to Charles Quint, courtesy of G.Dagli Orti, page 43

Material from the National Curriculum is Crown copyright and is reproduced with the permission of the controller of HMSO.

Editor: Gill Wilton (Campion Communications) and Edward Rippeth
Design: Andy Bailey
Layout artist: Patricia Hollingsworth
Cover image: Georgina Stein (picture) and Summayah Sadiq (writing)
Cover design: Andy Bailey/Alison Colver

© 1997 Folens Limited, on behalf of the author.
Every effort has been made to contact copyright holders of material used in this book. If any have been overlooked, we will be pleased to make any necessary arrangements.

First published 1997 by Folens Limited, Dunstable and Dublin.
Folens Limited, Albert House, Apex Business Centre, Boscombe Road, Dunstable, LU5 4RL, England.

ISBN 1 85276 964-5

Printed in Singapore by Craft Print

What is history?

Child – **'I wish I had been born in Victorian times.'**

Teacher – **'Why?'**

Child – **'Because then I wouldn't have so much history to remember!'**

Unlike the child above, we should aim to view history as more than remembering things that happened in the past. It is much more useful to consider it in terms of **knowledge**, **understanding** and **skills**.

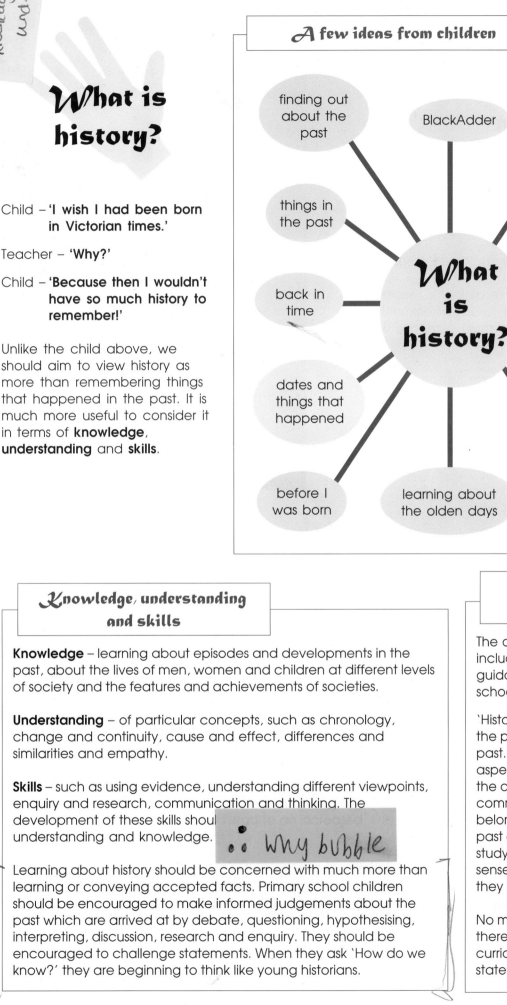

A few ideas from children

- finding out about the past
- BlackAdder
- things that people left behind
- things in the past
- stories about kings and queens
- **What is history?**
- back in time
- the past
- dates and things that happened
- things in museums
- before I was born
- learning about the olden days
- old people like my granny

Knowledge, understanding and skills

Knowledge – learning about episodes and developments in the past, about the lives of men, women and children at different levels of society and the features and achievements of societies.

Understanding – of particular concepts, such as chronology, change and continuity, cause and effect, differences and similarities and empathy.

Skills – such as using evidence, understanding different viewpoints, enquiry and research, communication and thinking. The development of these skills shou[ld be] understanding and knowledge.

Learning about history should be concerned with much more than learning or conveying accepted facts. Primary school children should be encouraged to make informed judgements about the past which are arrived at by debate, questioning, hypothesising, interpreting, discussion, research and enquiry. They should be encouraged to challenge statements. When they ask 'How do we know?' they are beginning to think like young historians.

Non-statutory guidance

The original history order included in the non-statutory guidance this definition of school history:

'History can mean two things: the past, and the study of the past. The past influences all aspects of our lives, it shapes the customs and beliefs of the communities to which we belong. Learning about the past and the methods used to study it helps pupils make sense of the world in which they live.'

No matter how many revisions there may be to the history curriculum in the future, this statement will always apply.

History in the National Curriculum
Key Stage 1

The National Curriculum for history consists of:
☞ programmes of study
☞ level descriptions for the attainment target.

Programmes of study contain all that is required for teaching, learning and day-to-day assessment. At Key Stage 1 there are three main components:

Key stage focus statement

Areas of study

Key elements

The attainment target sets out the expected standards of children's performance. You should be aware of the requirements before writing your scheme of work.

Key stage focus statement

What is its purpose?
☞ This statement sets out the objectives and provides a focus to teaching for the key stage as a whole. It summarises the main ways in which knowledge, understanding and skills should be developed in the key stage.

What is the focus statement?
☞ Pupils should be given opportunities to develop an awareness of the past and of the ways in which it was different from the present.
☞ They should be helped to set the study of the past in a chronological framework and to understand some of the ways in which we find out about the past.

Areas of study

What is their purpose?
☞ This section identifies the content to be taught which will provide a basis for study at Key Stage 1. It contains both specified content and criteria for content selection.

What are the areas of study?
☞ Everyday life, work, leisure and culture in the past.
☞ Changes in their own lives and those of their family or adults around them.
☞ Way of life of people in Britain in the past beyond living memory.
☞ Lives of famous men and women (including Britons).
☞ Past events of different types (including British).

Key elements

What is their purpose?
☞ This section characterises areas of progression in children's historical knowledge, understanding and skills. The key elements are closely related and should be developed through the areas of study. Not all key elements need to be developed in each area of study. More guidance is given on page 7.

What are the elements?
☞ Chronology
☞ Range and depth of historical knowledge and understanding
☞ Interpretation of history
☞ Historical enquiry
☞ Organisation and communication

A PRIMARY TEACHER'S HANDBOOK – *History*

Key elements in Key Stage 1

WHAT IT SAYS	KEY WORDS	WHAT IT MEANS
Children should be taught: (1a) To sequence events and objects in order to develop a sense of chronology;	**SEQUENCE**	Sort in order actual objects and pictures or photos of events and objects according to when they happened.
(1b) To use common words and phrases relating to the passing of time – old, new, before, after, long ago, days of the week, months, years;	**USE**	Develop and use a basic vocabulary which will help them to understand time.
(2a) About aspects of the past through stories from different periods and cultures, including stories and eye witness accounts of historical events;	**RECOGNISE**	Hear and read stories and first-hand accounts that will increase their knowledge of the past.
(2b) To recognise why people did things, why events happened and what happened as a result;	**RECOGNISE**	Begin to identify reasons and results of actions.
(2c) To identify differences between ways of life at different times;	**IDENTIFY**	Compare similarities and differences between then and now, and then and then.
(3a) To identify different ways in which the past is represented – pictures, written accounts, films, television programmes, plays, songs, reproductions of objects, museum displays;	**IDENTIFY**	Encounter and identify different sources and interpretations.
(4a) How to find out about aspects of the past from a range of sources of information, including artefacts, pictures and photographs, adults talking about their own past, written sources, and buildings and sites;	**FIND OUT**	Understand how to find out about the past from objects, pictorial and written sources, people and buildings.
(4b) To ask and answer questions about the past;	**ASK AND ANSWER**	Ask questions about sources and provide answers as part of their enquiry.
(5a) To communicate their awareness and understanding of history in a variety of ways.	**COMMUNICATE**	Use a variety of recording and presentation methods.

History in the National Curriculum
Key Stage 2

Churches and cathedrals provide a rich source of historical evidence.

The programmes of study contain all that is required for teaching, learning and day-to-day assessment. The Key Stage 2 Programme of Study consists of three main components:

Key stage focus statement

Study units

Key elements

Key stage focus statement

What is its purpose?
☛ This statement provides a focus for teaching and learning across the key stage. It also identifies the main ways in which children's knowledge, understanding and skills are expected to develop in the key stage.

What is the focus statement?
☛ Pupils should be taught about important episodes and developments in Britain's past, from Roman to modern times, about ancient civilisations and the history of other parts of the world. They should be helped to develop a chronological framework by making links across the different study units. They should have opportunities to investigate local history and to learn about the past from a range of sources of information.

Study units

What is their purpose?
☛ This section identifies the historical content which provides a basis for study at Key Stage 2. A detailed specification of content is provided in each of the six study units. The opportunities that should be given to children for the study of certain aspects and perspectives is also included.

What are the study units?
☛ Romans, Anglo-Saxons and Vikings in Britain
☛ Life in Tudor times
☛ Victorian Britain **or** Britain since 1930
☛ Ancient Greece
☛ Local history
☛ A past non-European society

Plus
☛ Aspects in outline and depth
☛ Aspects of the histories of England, Ireland, Scotland and Wales
☛ Variety of perspectives

Key elements

What is their purpose?
☛ This section characterises areas of progression in children's historical knowledge, understanding and skills. The key elements apply across the key stage and should be developed through the study units. Not all key elements need to be developed in each study unit. More guidance is given on page 9.

What are the key elements?
☛ Chronology
☛ Range and depth of historical knowledge and understanding
☛ Interpretation of history
☛ Historical enquiry
☛ Organisation and communication

A PRIMARY TEACHER'S HANDBOOK – *History*

Key elements in Key Stage 2

WHAT IT SAYS	KEY WORDS	WHAT IT MEANS
Children should be taught: (1a) To place events, people and changes in the periods studied within a chronological framework.	SEQUENCE	Sequence aspects within and between study units.
(1b) To use dates and terms relating to the passing of time, including ancient, modern, BC and AD, century and decade, and which define different periods – Tudor, Victorian.	USE	Use a more sophisticated time vocabulary related to study units.
(2a) About characteristic features of particular periods and societies, including the ideas, beliefs and attitudes of people in the past, and the experiences of men and women; and about the social, cultural, religious and ethnic diversity of the societies studied.	UNDERSTAND	Understand characteristic features, including experiences and beliefs of all members of society.
(2b) To describe and identify reasons for and results of historical events, situations and changes both within and across periods.	DESCRIBE AND IDENTIFY	Understand why something happened or changed and what the results were.
(2c) To describe and make links between the main events, situations and changes both within and across periods.	DESCRIBE AND LINK	Make connections and understand links within and between study units.
(3a) To identify and give reasons for different ways in which the past is represented and interpreted.	IDENTIFY AND SUGGEST	Identify and give reasons for different interpretations.
(4a) How to find out about aspects of the period studied from a range of sources of information, including documents and printed sources, artefacts, pictures and photographs, music and buildings and sites.	FIND OUT	Understand how to find out about the past from written and pictorial sources, objects, music and buildings.
(4b) To ask and answer questions, and to select and record information relevant to a topic.	ASK AND ANSWER	Ask questions of sources and consider usefulness and relevance to their work.
(5a) To recall, select and organise historical information, including dates and terms.	RECALL, SELECT AND ORGANISE	Develop recall and research skills.
(5b) The terms necessary to describe the periods and topics studied, including court, monarch, parliament, nation, civilisation, invasion, conquest, settlement, conversion, slavery, trade, industry, law.	RECALL, SELECT AND ORGANISE	Use specific terms in correct context.
(5c) To communicate their knowledge and understanding in a variety of ways, including structured narrative and descriptions.	COMMUNICATE	Use a variety of recording and presentation methods.

Writing a whole-school policy

These two pages offer guidelines on writing a policy and suggest a possible format on which to base your own policy.

Policy and plans have an important relationship. Planning should be informed by policy and all policy should be evident in plans. If a policy contains the statement 'We believe that history should be taught through first-hand contact with artefacts, pictorial and written evidence', then plans (and practice!) should show this.

A policy should outline your belief and approach to current and future practice. It is part of a school's response to questions of accountability and provides governors, OFSTED, LEAs and parents with evidence of a school's vision and intentions. But the most important purpose of a policy is to assure and promote quality teaching and learning. It ensures that the same messages and procedures are understood and practised by all.

The co-ordinator should write and steer the policy from its conception to approval by the governing body, but all the staff need to feel ownership of the document if it is to result in a change in practice. All staff should understand that they have a corporate responsibility to implement the decisions within the policy. Any disagreements should be aired during development and a consensus reached.

Policies kept on disc are easier to update. It is also easier if the document is kept in a loose-leaf file instead of being bound, so single pages may be changed.

Policy writing in stages

Stage one
Audit any existing documents, plans and current practice. Consider timescale for policy writing. Action plan for each stage and financial implications.

Stage two
Seek advice and support from:
colleagues
other policies
LEA
other schools.
Is there a school format for policies to follow?

Stage three
Write out headings for each section of policy. Brainstorm ideas to be included. Write first draft.

Stage four
Present first draft to staff for discussion. Check whether everything needs to be included. For example, is there a separate policy for differentiation that repeats what you have said?

Stage five
Amend draft and write copy for staff and governors to agree and approve. Add heading with details of when written, by whom, when approved and plans for review.

Stage six
Consider who has copies and where kept. Launch and implement policy. Decide criteria for success. Monitor success.

Is your policy ...

☞ written in simple language?
☞ a reflection of the aims, philosophy and principles of whole school policy?
☞ dated?
☞ a commitment to quality teaching and learning?
☞ a commitment to raising standards in history?
☞ user friendly and useable?
☞ written in such a way that a new member of staff would understand the school's approach?
☞ agreed and supported by all staff?
☞ used?

Elements of a history policy

There are usually two parts to a policy document: a policy statement and the guidelines.

Policy statement

This is a public document that should be available for interested parties, such as parents, to read. It describes the general guiding principles and should include:

☛ **Aims** A statement on your approach and general philosophy. What is history? What is good history practice at your school?

☛ **Objectives** How the school will achieve its aims in relation to the National Curriculum.

☛ **Delivery** How the subject is delivered, whether through topic work, as a separate subject or by using a particular scheme and the contribution of history to the discretionary 20 per cent of the curriculum.

☛ **Time** An indication of the approximate amount of time to be allocated.

Guidelines

These are not a public document. They should offer professional support for the teachers in your school and give advice on the planning and implementation of the principles specified in the policy statement. They should include:

☛ **Planning advice** Guidelines on how to plan from the learning objectives at medium- and short-term level and a copy of the scheme of work (the long-term plan).

☛ **Teaching and learning** Advice on some teaching styles and learning activities. Certain areas of history may need specific advice, for example approaches to teaching chronology.

☛ **Progression** How progression in knowledge, understanding and skills can be developed.

☛ **Differentiation** Advice on appropriate strategies and when best employed. Ideas for very able and special needs children.

☛ **Assessment recording and reporting** Advice on formative assessment and record-keeping procedures, school portfolios of children's work and moderation.

☛ **Resources** Information concerning the storage and retrieval of resources, advice on particular ones, possible visits and fieldwork, setting up class museums. Financial allocation.

☛ **Equal opportunities** How this will be addressed.

☛ **Co-ordinator's role** A statement on the role and responsibilities, including monitoring.

☛ **Quality assurance** How the policy and practice will be evaluated and monitored, by whom and when.

An example of a policy statement

We believe history to be the study of people in the past and how their actions have affected our lives today. History can help children to make sense of the world in which they live and help them develop a sense of identity. Good practice is demonstrated by children being actively involved in the study of the past, using a range of sources of information, asking questions such as 'How do we know?' and making progress. We will achieve these broad aims by the following objectives:

☛ To develop an awareness of the past and of the ways in which it was different from the present.

☛ To understand how we find out about the past.

☛ To develop a chronological framework for time periods studied.

☛ To consider history from a variety of perspectives – political, economic, technological and scientific, social, religious, cultural and aesthetic.

☛ To begin to understand why some aspects of the past are subject to different interpretations.

☛ To arouse children's interest in the past and stimulate their curiosity into finding out more by research and enquiry.

At Key Stage 1, history is taught through a topic approach with a main history focus twice each year. At Key Stage 2, history is taught as a subject. In Key Stage 1, approximately 72 hours over the key stage are allocated to history. In Key Stage 2, 180 hours are allocated. At present, one hour a week of our school's discretionary 20 per cent is spent on history.

Writing a scheme of work

A scheme of work should be a long-term overview of how the history programmes of study will be covered at your school. It should form the basis for your medium- and short-term planning. It should demonstrate how other aspects, such as continuity and progression, will be ensured.

The flow diagram on this page shows the stages of development of a scheme of work. On the following pages are guidelines on the medium-term and long-term planning that comprises the scheme of work. Finally, there is a checklist below against which you should test your scheme of work.

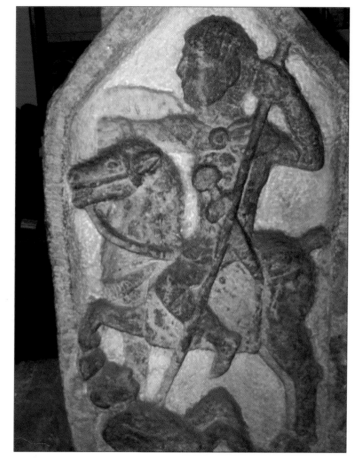

A Roman soldier's tombstone.

Writing a scheme of work in stages

Does your scheme of work:

- specify the content to be taught in each year group?

- identify a clear focus for learning within each unit work/content block?

- demonstrate how progression will be ensured across the key stage(s)?

- allocate a notional time to teach and assess work?

- sequence the work to ensure a balance in the key stage and within each year?

Stage one
Allocate content (whole study units in Key Stage 2 or parts of different areas of study in Key Stage 1) to each year group. Sequence over three terms. Consider whether any extra history will be taught.

Stage two
Identify the focus for learning within each of these blocks of content.

Stage three
Allocate the key elements to be developed within the content.

Stage four
Check coverage of all key elements. Ensure progression of key elements across key stage.

Stage five
Ensure work is sequenced and balanced across the key stage. Ensure consideration is given to links with other curriculum areas when appropriate.

Stage six
Allocate an approximate amount of time to be spent on each unit of history.

A PRIMARY TEACHER'S HANDBOOK – *History*

Key Stage 1

The key elements should be developed through the areas of study as appropriate. However, not all the key elements need to be developed in each area of study. The following stages will help you to plan the development of key elements:

Decide on topic titles and organisation of content from the areas of study.

Consider the most appropriate key elements to be developed with the proposed content.

Complete a matrix like the one on the next page to ensure coverage of all key elements.

Prepare your long-term plan for the key stage (see page 15).

Prepare a medium-term plan for each history topic, demonstrating how each proposed key element is linked to the content (see Unit of Work Planning Sheet, page 16).

Medium-term plan

☞ The medium-term plan should show how each unit of work is broken down into individual teaching and learning sessions. The starting point for each session should be the learning objectives – the purpose of the lesson and what you want the children to know, understand or do. The next stage is to consider a key question to be answered and activities that will deliver the learning objective. Assessment will be in terms of how successful the children are in achieving this learning objective. Planning should not start from an activity with an appropriate learning objective coming as an afterthought.

☞ With the revised order for history, all the learning objectives should come from the programme of study. This means that each learning objective for a particular activity should combine an aspect of a key element with an aspect of content from an area of study. For example, the second key question from the Key Stage 1 plan for *Our School* is 'What happens in a school day and a school year?' The learning objective, which should be the starting point for this question and the activity, combines Key Elements 1a and 1b – Chronology: 'Pupils should be taught:

● to sequence events

● to use common words and phrases relating to the passing of time – before, after, days of week, months, years ...

With the Area of Study 1a: Pupils should be taught about –

● changes in their own lives ...'

Each teaching and learning activity should therefore combine at least one learning objective from the key elements with one aspect of content. Key Element 5, Organisation and communication, may run throughout every taught unit of history.

A PRIMARY TEACHER'S HANDBOOK – *History*

Key Stage 1 History topic titles	Coverage of key elements								
	1a	*1b*	*2a*	*2b*	*2c*	*3a*	*4a*	*4b*	*5*
Reception									
Year 1									
Year 2									
Extra history as part of the 20 per cent	*1a*	*1b*	*2a*	*2b*	*2c*	*3a*	*4a*	*4b*	*5*

Key Stage 1

Long-term overview for History

	Reception	Year 1	Year 2
Autumn		**Famous person or event** *Time allocation:* 2 hours *Key Element focus:* 2a, 4a, 4b *Area of Study focus:* 2, 3	**Our school and local area** *Time allocation:* 14 hours *Key Element focus:* 1a, 2b, 2c, 3a, 4a, 5 *Area of Study focus:* 1a, 1b
		Toys and Christmas – then and now *Time allocation:* 12 hours *Key Element focus:* 1b, 2a, 2c, 4a, 5 *Area of Study focus:* 1a, 1b	**Famous person or event** *Time allocation:* 2 hours *Key Element focus:* 2a, 4a, 4b *Area of Study focus:* 2, 3
Spring	**Me and my family** *Time allocation:* 10 hours *Key Element focus:* 1a, 4b, 5a *Area of Study focus:* 1a	**Grannies and grandads** *Time allocation:* 12 hours *Key Element focus:* 1a, 2a, 2b, 4b *Area of Study focus:* 1a, 1b	
	Famous person or event *Time allocation:* 2 hours *Key Element focus:* 2a, 4a, 4b *Area of Study focus:* 2, 3		**Living in a castle** *Time allocation:* 14 hours *Key Element focus:* 1b, 2a, 2b, 2c, 3a, 4b, 5 *Area of Study focus:* 1a, 1b
Summer	**My home and my school** *Time allocation:* 10 hours *Key Element focus:* 1a, 4a, 4b *Area of Study focus:* 1a	**Underground** *Time allocation:* 6 hours *Key Element focus:* 1a, 3a, 4a, 5 *Area of Study focus:* 1a, 1b	
	Famous person or event *Time allocation:* 2 hours *Key Element focus:* 2a, 4a, 4b *Area of Study focus:* 2, 3	**Famous person or event** *Time allocation:* 2 hours *Key Element focus:* 2a, 4a, 4b *Area of Study focus:* 2, 3	**Holidays and journeys** *Time allocation:* 8 hours *Key Element focus:* 1a, 1b, 2c, 3a, 5 *Area of Study focus:* 1a, 1b

Unit of work planning sheet

Curriculum area: History – Our School

NB: Aspects of Key Element 5, Organisation and Communication, will run throughout the unit.

Year/Class _____   Date/term _____

Key questions/issues	Activities	Learning objectives/ Criteria for assessment
What does the first day at school feel like? How do we know?	Read stories and talk about a child's first day at school. Can the children remember one good thing/bad thing? Similarities/differences between life now and pre-school.	– identify differences between ways of life at different times – use common words and phrases relating to the passing of time – before, after – learn about changes in their own lives
What happens in a school day and school year?	Sequence the school day and school year, and photos of school events. Play games where wrong sequencing has to be corrected.	– sequence events – use common words and phrases relating to the passing of time – days of week, months, years – learn about changes in their own lives
Who works in our school?	People in school community talk about their work, how long they have been working there and any changes that have taken place. Record their involvement with school on a time-line. Collect evidence belonging to people in school community – children guess who it belongs to.	– find out about aspects of the past from artefacts, adults and buildings – sequence events – find out about changes in the lives of adults around them – ask and answer questions about the past
How can we find out about the history of our school?	Explore old photos, log books. Teachers and pupils to find out about school. Make a class museum/display about school. Children to write/word process labels for exhibits.	– find out about everyday life in the past, for example education – find out about aspects of the past beyond living memory – find out about the past from a range of sources of information
What were schools like 100 years ago?	Use photographs of old classroom. Children (in pairs) ask and answer questions about photo. ● What can I see for certain? ● What can I make a sensible guess about? ● What would I like to find out more about? Compare with classrooms of today.	– find out about the past from a range of sources of information – ask and answer questions about the past – identify between ways of life and different times
How can we tell people in the future about our class/school?	Collect for a Museum of the Future that would tell people about life today. Children to draw/write brochures for museum or make tape to describe exhibits.	– find out about the past from a range of sources of information – ask and answer questions about the past

A PRIMARY TEACHER'S HANDBOOK – *History*

Key Stage 2

Key Stage 2 requires a similar planning procedure to the one outlined for Key Stage 1. The main difference will be that schools need to make decisions about which aspects of the past to study in outline and in depth. To aid progression, the key elements at Key Stage 2 are more complex and challenging. Complete a matrix similar to the one on the next page to help ensure coverage of all aspects.

Recreating a village shop in the classroom.

Decide on the order of study units and make choices where necessary.

⬇

Consider the most appropriate key elements to be developed with the proposed content.

⬇

Complete a matrix like the one on the next page to ensure coverage of all key elements.

⬇

Prepare your long-term plan for the key stage (see page 19).

⬇

Prepare a medium-term plan for each history topic, demonstrating how each proposed key element is linked to content (see Unit of Work Planning Sheet, page 20).

Medium-term plan

☛ The medium-term plan should demonstrate how each study unit at Key Stage 2 will be taught over a series of teaching sessions. Like Key Stage 1 it should contain:
- learning objectives
- teaching and learning activities.

It may also contain details of:
- resources (although this information may be in the relevant study unit resource box)
- differentiation and classroom organisation (although this information may be included in short-term weekly or daily plans).

☛ Each learning objective should combine an aspect of the key elements with an aspect of content from the study unit. For example, the key question from the medium-term plan for leisure in Victorian Britain is, 'How did the Victorians spend their leisure time?'.

☛ The learning objectives from the key elements are 2a and 4a.
'Pupils should be taught:
- to find out about aspects of the periods studied from a range of sources of information
- about characteristic features of the Victorian period.'

☛ The learning objective from the content in the study units is that children should be taught about:
- the lives of people at different levels of society in town and country
- leisure in Victorian times, for example, music, sport, holidays, and the Great Exhibition.

☛ Some aspects of Key Element 5, Organisation and Communication, may run throughout the whole study unit.

Key Stage 2 study units	Coverage of key elements										
	1a	*1b*	*2a*	*2b*	*2c*	*3a*	*4a*	*4b*	*5a*	*5b*	*5c*
1 Romans, Anglo-Saxons and Vikings in Britain											
2 Life in Tudor times											
3a Victorian Britain **or** 3b Britain since 1930											
4 Ancient Greece											
5 Local history											
6 A past non-European society											
Extra history as part of the 20%											

A PRIMARY TEACHER'S HANDBOOK – *History*

Key Stage 2

Long-term overview for History

	Year 3	Year 4	Year 5	Year 6
Autumn	**Ancient Egypt** *Time allocation:* 30 hours *Key Element focus:* 1a, 1b, 2a, 4b, 5a, 5b, 5c *Study Unit focus:* The way of life, beliefs and achievements of the ancient Egyptians and their legacy to the modern world.		**Life in Tudor Times** *Time allocation:* 30 hours *Key Element focus:* 1a, 2b, 4a, 4b, 5a, 5b, 5c *Study Unit focus:* Some of the major events and personalities, such as monarchs, and the way of life of people at different levels of society in Tudor times.	
Spring		**Romans, Anglo-Saxons and Vikings in Britain** Overview and Roman focus *Time allocation:* 30 hours *Key Element focus:* 1a, 3a, 4a, 5a, 5b, 5c *Study Unit focus:* History of British Isles from 55BC to early 11th century and the ways in which British society was shaped by different peoples.		**Local history** Focus on impact of WW2 on the locality. *Time allocation:* 30 hours *Key Element focus:* 1a, 2c, 3a, 4a, 5a, 5b, 5c *Study Unit focus:* An aspect of the local community during a short period of time or the local community's involvement in a particular event.
Summer	**Ancient Greece** *Time allocation:* 30 hours *Key Element focus:* 1a, 1b, 2a, 4a, 4b, 5a, 5b, 5c *Study Unit focus:* The way of life, beliefs and achievements of the ancient Greeks and the legacy of ancient Greek civilisation to the modern world.		**Victorian Britain** *Time allocation:* 30 hours *Key Element focus:* 1a, 2a, 2b, 2c, 4a, 4b, 5a, 5b, 5c *Study Unit focus:* The lives of men, women and children at different levels of society in Britain and how they were affected by changes in industry and transport.	

Unit of work planning sheet

Curriculum area: History – Victorian Britain

Year/Class _____   Date/term _____

Key questions and issues	Activities	Learning objectives/ Criteria for assessment
When did the Victorians live? How do we know about them?	Teacher presentation using time-line or family tree to demonstrate 'How long ago?' Class to list/brainstorm possible sources, teacher to collect examples and display in class museum. Children to write/word-process labels for museum collection.	– to place events and people within a chronological framework – to use dates and terms that define a period, e.g. Victorian – to find out about the past from a range of sources of information – to learn about Victoria and the Royal Family – to find out about the past from written/pictorial sources
Who was Queen Victoria? How did she live and reign?	Give different images of Victoria to pairs/groups of children. Ask them to describe them and feed this back to class. Discuss deficiencies of evidence with the class. Sequence images, put on time-line. Teacher input – Victoria's life and family tree.	– to learn about Victoria and the royal family – to find out about the past from written/pictorial sources
What was life like for different Victorian families?	Various photos, interpretations of Victorian family life. Children to describe their picture without seeing others (deficiency of evidence). Give background information from documentary sources. Investigate usefulness of all sources used. Consider roles of servants.	– to learn about family life at different levels of society – to find out about the past from pictorial/documentary evidence
What was life like for Victorian children at school?	Role-play Victorian school day. (Use *History in Evidence* pack). Research from original photos, other sources. List differences/similarities between then and now. Extended writing – a school inspector describing a visit to school.	– to learn about life in school using a range of sources – to make comparisons with other periods – to identify how the past is interpreted
What was life like for working children?	Role-play, interviews in pairs. One as working child, other the investigator concerned with working conditions. Present to the rest of the class.	– to learn about lives of children at work – to research using documentary evidence and interpretations – to make own interpretations – to ask and answer questions
What happened to poor people?	Show a short extract of workhouse scene from *Oliver*. Discuss what it would have been like there. Research site of local Victorian workhouse. Use plans/description to investigate conditions. Make gruel. Extended writing – a diary entry 'Entering the workhouse'.	– to research using a range of sources – to ask and answer questions – to find out about lives of poor people in town and country, including workhouses, reforms and Sunday schools

A PRIMARY TEACHER'S HANDBOOK – *History*

A busy high street in late Victorian Luton.

Recreating Victorian children at play.

Key questions/issues	Activities	Learning objectives/ Criteria for assessment
How and why did Victorian towns grow?	Investigate local Victorian maps that illustrate development of railways, growth of towns. List changes and reasons for them. Investigate/sketch local Victorian houses. Record Victorian buildings on present day map of local area.	– to describe and identify reasons for events and changes – to research from a range of sources: maps, photographs, buildings – to select and record relevant information
Why did industry and transport change in Victorian times?	Consideration of transport/industry in Victorian times. List/sequence changes. Match to reasons for changes.	– to learn how changes in industry and transport affected the lives of Victorian people – to give reasons for changes
How did the Victorians spend their leisure time?	Variety of sources depicting leisure. Who would have enjoyed these activities? How were they different from today? What did Victorian children do in their leisure time? Research from sources. Present in form of newspaper article or advert for leisure activity. Learn songs from music halls.	– to learn about leisure: music, sport, holidays, the Great Exhibition – to use a range of sources – to learn about characteristic features of Victorian period
How and why did the British Empire grow?	Teacher input and map of world showing Empire, imports and exports, immigration and emigration, plus extracts showing Victorian attitudes to the world. Compare to today. Consider pros/cons of British Empire for Britain and other countries.	– to identify reasons for events, situations and changes in Victorian times
What achievements were the Victorians proud of?	Groups to focus on one aspect – inventions, discoveries, buildings, art, photography, architecture, literature. Group research and present findings to rest of class.	– to ask and answer questions, select and record information relevant to a topic

Progression through the key elements

Chronology

Nursery/Reception

Considers differences between him/herself as a baby and as he/she is now. Sorts pictures and objects between those related to babies, children and adults.

Uses simple time-lines to sequence from their own experience. Considers differences and changes over time.

Sequences within clock and calendar time – within a day, a week, seasons and school year.

Shows an awareness of different parts of stories and begins to sequence parts of stories required by the programme of study.

Stone plaques often pinpoint dates of events, such as a school being built.

Develops awareness of BC/AD, ancient and modern in context of all study units being taught.

Places Study Units within century(ies). Able to place events in study units more precisely on time-lines.

Progresses sequencing from within their own memory to within living memory of others – parents and grandparents. Begins to justify sequencing and understand that needs change over time.

Develops an understanding of the duration of time. Uses terms to define period being studied.

Begins to associate dates with particular people and events.

Sequences evidence from different periods of time, including a time period in the past beyond living memory, and is able to justify sequencing.

Year 6

Develops an awareness of dates and begins to use the terms decade and century. Able to sequence evidence and their own recorded work on time-lines related to a study unit.

A PRIMARY TEACHER'S HANDBOOK – *History*

Range and depth of historical knowledge and understanding

Nursery/Reception

Demonstrates some understanding of past events as told in stories.

Compares similarities and differences between then and now.

Listens to a range of stories that illustrate aspects of the past.

Identifies reasons and the results of their own actions.

Reads and understands information about past events.

Begins to identify reasons and results of actions in the past.

Compares similarities and differences between different historical periods in the past.

Makes connections between and compares different historical periods.

Makes connections and understands links between developments within a study unit.

Understands why something happened and changed and what the results were.

Describes different features of an historical period.

Year 6

Interpretations of history

Nursery/Reception

Relates their account of an incident or event in school and begins to understand that other children may give a different version.

Recognises in a class display that interpretations of people and events in a time period studied come in various forms.

Knows that a familiar event, such as a school play, can be represented in different ways – pictures, photos, video or newspaper report.

Contributes to a class discussion or brainstorm session, listing different interpretations – films, books, pictures, plays.

An early Victorian-style living room.

When on educational visits, recognises that museum displays and reconstructions are someone's interpretation of what happened or what things might have looked like.

Knows and begins to use the terms 'interpretation' and 'version'. Begins to understand that they are attempts by later people to explain what it was like then.

Asks questions such as, 'Why were the interpretations produced?', 'Why do people interpret events in different ways?' and offers answers.

Understands that their own personal interpretation of the past, such as a picture of Boudicca drawn from the written description, should be included when considering different types of interpretations.

Demonstrates an understanding that interpretations are produced for a range of different purposes – to amuse, to educate.

Compares different interpretations of an event or group of people, eg describes contrasting pictorial interpretations of the Vikings, and considers the different image that each might intend to portray.

Researches and collects several interpretations related to time period being studied.

Year 6

A PRIMARY TEACHER'S HANDBOOK – *History*

Historical enquiry

Uses sources to make comparisons between life then and now.

Nursery/Reception

Uses senses to describe the physical appearance of sources.

Begins to ask and answer questions about the use, function and construction of sources.

Is familiar with a range of sources and recognises that they are clues that help us find out about the past.

Begins to make deductions from sources.

Is familiar with a wide range of evidence related to the period studied.

Realises that there may be a deficiency of evidence when using sources and that they may need to find their answers elsewhere.

Considers the usefulness and reliability of all sources of information used.

Chooses relevant information from sources to answer questions.

Uses more difficult sources of information, particularly documents and printed sources.

Selects the most useful sources of information for their enquiries.

Year 6

Organisation and communication

Re-tells accounts of past events and stories of famous men and women.

Nursery/Reception

Talks about their own history and their own memories of past events.

Talks, draws or writes about aspects of the past taught from the Areas of Study.

Year 6

Obtains information from sources and communicates it by using different forms of extended writing – diaries, journals, letters.

Uses IT to organise, display and interpret numerical information graphically. Carries out simple searches on a prepared database. Prepares information to add to the file.

A PRIMARY TEACHER'S HANDBOOK – *History*

Reports what they have found out about a topic.

Uses a word processor to produce work, such as labels for a class museum. Presents in a bar graph or pie chart information obtained, for example through interview or their own reading.

Plans a group/class display on an aspect of a Study Unit and selects relevant information.

Shows an understanding of an event or story through mime, dance or role-play.

Plans, drafts and refines narratives and descriptions of the past (word-processed and written).

Uses, in speech and writing, the correct terms to describe the period or topic being studied.

Researches different viewpoints and takes part in a debate about a past event.

Level descriptions

Each of the eight level descriptions gives an overview of the type and range of performance that children working at this level should demonstrate.

They should be used to make a judgement about all aspects of a child's performance against the key features described in the level descriptions. They are not designed for teaching and learning objectives or day-to-day assessment.

The level descriptions should only be used when attainment needs to be summarised and reported on at a particular point.

What does 'best fit' mean?

Each level description is meant to be a 'best fit' description. This means that the descriptions are intended to be viewed holistically, not split up into different phrases or sentences to be used as a basis for a checklist. However, many schools have started doing just this as a means of:
– helping them to become more familiar with each level description
– helping them to become more confident at making 'best fit' judgements
– helping them to identify gaps in their coverage of the key elements or content.

The following pages contain examples of individual and class record sheets. Page 29 can be used as a class record and provides an overview of the whole class's attainment. Page 30 is an individual record; a similar one should be drawn up for Key Stage 2. Page 31 is a long-term record of achievement. A similar one would need to be provided for Key Stage 1.

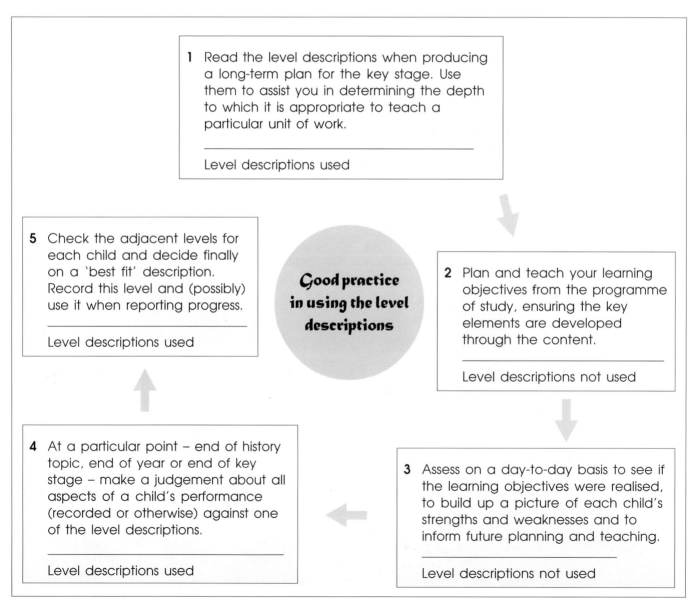

1 Read the level descriptions when producing a long-term plan for the key stage. Use them to assist you in determining the depth to which it is appropriate to teach a particular unit of work.

Level descriptions used

Good practice in using the level descriptions

2 Plan and teach your learning objectives from the programme of study, ensuring the key elements are developed through the content.

Level descriptions not used

3 Assess on a day-to-day basis to see if the learning objectives were realised, to build up a picture of each child's strengths and weaknesses and to inform future planning and teaching.

Level descriptions not used

4 At a particular point – end of history topic, end of year or end of key stage – make a judgement about all aspects of a child's performance (recorded or otherwise) against one of the level descriptions.

Level descriptions used

5 Check the adjacent levels for each child and decide finally on a 'best fit' description. Record this level and (possibly) use it when reporting progress.

Level descriptions used

A PRIMARY TEACHER'S HANDBOOK – *History* © Folens (not copiable)

Class record sheet – History

Curriculum area: History –

Year/Class _____ **Date/Term** _____ **Topic/Study Unit** _____

At the end of each history topic/study unit, please judge the knowledge, understanding and skills demonstrated by each pupil and place them against a level. Remember they are 'best fit' descriptions.

Level descriptions	Best fit pupils
Level 1 Distinguish between present and past in own and other's lives. Sequence events and objects. Know and recount episodes from stories about past. Find answers to questions from sources of information.	
Level 2 Use terms concerned with time passing, order events and objects and distinguish between today and the past. Show knowledge and understanding of aspects of the past before living memory. Recognise there are reasons why people acted as they did. Identify ways in which the past is shown. Answer questions from sources on the basis of simple observations.	
Level 3 Show increasing awareness that the past can be divided into different periods, recognise similarities and differences between them. Show knowledge and understanding of some of the events, people and changes from the appropriate programme of study. Start to give reasons for, and results of, events and changes. Identify ways in which the past is represented. Answer questions by using sources in ways beyond simple observations.	
Level 4 Show knowledge and understanding of aspects of history of Britain and other countries. Describe past societies and periods and identify changes within and across them. Describe events, people and changes and give some reasons for, and results of them. Show different interpretations. Select and combine information from sources. Produce structured work, making use of dates and terms.	
Level 5 Show an increasing depth of knowledge and understanding of history of Britain and other countries. Describe and make links between past societies and periods. Describe and make links between, relevant reasons for and results of, events and changes. Suggest reasons for different interpretations. Evaluate, select and organise sources to produce structured work.	**Date completed**

Key Stage 1 History – Individual record

Name: _____

Highlight aspects of the level descriptions which best describe the child's performance at the end of each topic.

    Year 1 to be completed in red.
    Year 2 to be completed in blue.
    Please record in the Year 1/Year 2 boxes any **significant** rapid, or lack of, progress.

Level 1
Pupils recognise the distinction between present and past in their own and others' lives. They begin to show a sense of chronology by placing a few events and objects in sequence, and by using everyday terms about passing time. They know and retell stories about the past. They begin to use sources.

Level 2
Pupils use terms concerned with time passing, order events and objects, and distinguish between areas of their own lives and the past. They show knowledge and understanding of aspects of the past beyond living memory, and of some of the events and people they have studied. They begin to recognise that there are reasons why people in the past acted as they did. They begin to identify some of the ways in which the past is represented. They answer questions about the past, from sources of information, on the basis of simple observations.

Level 3
Pupils show understanding of chronology by increasing awareness that history can be divided into different periods. They recognise some of the similarities and differences between periods and they use dates and terms. They demonstrate factual knowledge and understanding of some historical events, people and changes. They begin to give a few reasons for, and results of, the events and changes. They identify some different ways in which the past is represented. They find answers about the past using sources of information in ways beyond simple observations.

Year 1	Year 2

Summary History record sheet for

_____

At the end of each Study Unit, please comment on significant progress or lack of it, plus 'best fit' level description.

		Ancient Egypt	
Year 3			
Year 4	Romans, Anglo-Saxons and Vikings in Britain		Ancient Greece
Year 5		Life in Tudor times	
Year 6	Local history		Victorian Britain

Early years history

Knowledge and understanding of the world is one of the six areas of learning which SCAA has advised very young children should be introduced to. This will provide them with a foundation for later achievements. For History, children should talk about where they live, their families and past and present events in their lives. On the right are a few suggestions as to how this might be carried out.

Planning

It is important to plan with a particular learning objective in mind. Below is an example of a plan for use with a particular story in Early Years History.

Home corner

Set up a home corner with old objects and clothes, household equipment, books and toys. Let the children dress up and play in the 'old house'. What is similar to or different from their homes today?

Stories

Read on the theme of change or growth. Discuss the idea that needs change as we grow older.

Time-lines

The children could draw, on simple prepared concertina books, three pictures of themselves in sequence – as a baby, as a toddler and as they are now. Alternatively they could peg on a washing line clothes that they wore at different ages. Can they put them in the right order?

People

Talk about special days and events in your own childhood. What special days and events are important in their lives? Can they draw them or tell you about them?

Sorting exercise

Sort a collection of objects (toys, clothes or books) into two groups – those they used/played with as a baby and those they use now.
☛ How are they different?
☛ How are they similar?

Key questions/issues	Activities	Learning objectives
What was life like for the granny in the story when she was little?	Group listens to teacher reading the story *When I was Little* by M Williams.	– begin to understand that the past is no longer with us but that we can find out about it from stories and people
Was life different then to today?	Teacher questions children about similarities and differences. Children could draw these and they could be recorded in a class poster.	– begin to identify differences between then and now
How can we find out about our grannies' lives when they were little?	Class discussion to consider how we find out – ask our grannies, look at old photos. Ask a granny to talk to the class about their childhood.	– begin to understand that we find out about the past from evidence – the clues left behind

Resources

When I was Little M Williams (Walker Books).
Photographs of different aspects of life of a granny – school, holidays, home life.

𝒰sing evidence

Using evidence to find out about the past is a requirement of Key Element 4 – Historical Enquiry. Children should be made aware that evidence provides clues about things that happened in the past. Historians use evidence to construct a picture of the past.

A recreation of a Viking family home, while father's out raiding (at the Jorvik Viking Centre, York).

𝒲here can evidence be found?

Evidence can be found in sources. There are two main types of sources – primary and secondary.
☞ **Primary sources** These are always original or first hand from the time in question – direct testimony from an eye witness, diaries, log books, portraits and photographs. The further you go back in time, the fewer primary sources are available.
☞ **Secondary sources** These are based on primary sources and are produced after the event. Therefore evidence is always second-hand evidence is: history text books, biographies and reconstructions.

𝒲hich sources should be used?

The following range of sources is required by the National Curriculum:

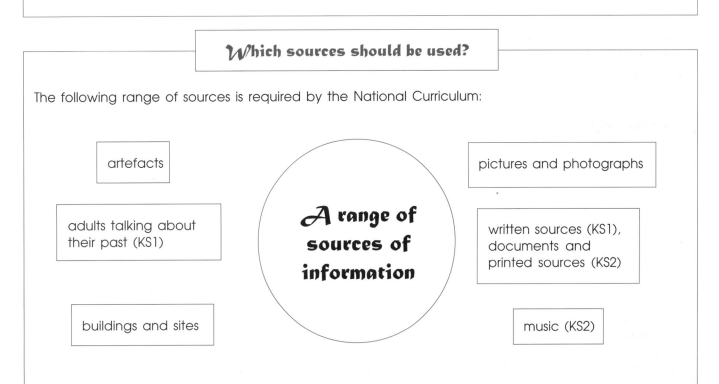

artefacts

adults talking about their past (KS1)

buildings and sites

𝒜 range of sources of information

pictures and photographs

written sources (KS1), documents and printed sources (KS2)

music (KS2)

Learning from artefacts

In both key stages, children are required to find out about aspects of the past from artefacts. Artefacts or objects provide children with an opportunity to handle primary sources. Almost every artefact is capable of teaching them something about life at a particular time and the technology of the era.

Why use artefacts?

☛ Handling artefacts motivates children and stimulates their curiosity.

☛ Artefacts provide something tangible to touch and work with.

☛ Using artefacts makes children aware at an early age that history is a process of enquiry and that they are working in the same way as historians.

☛ They remove the barrier of the written word. All children can use artefacts.

☛ Many important skills are furthered by using artefacts, especially speaking and listening.

☛ They encourage children to ask questions which lead to further research. It helps them to realise that because some parts may be missing or broken they should be wary when making their conclusions.

Activities with artefacts

Sorting and sequencing

☛ Sort the objects into two groups – those used today and those used in the past.

☛ Classify them into different categories, for example, things a child or an adult would use.

☛ Sequence objects on time-lines of varying difficulty.

Making deductions

☛ Use clues from close observation of objects to work out more information and give a reason to support their deduction.

☛ Set out the deduction in spoken or written words – 'I think ... because ... '

Close observation

☛ Make detailed labelled sketches of objects.

☛ Work in pairs sitting back to back. One child describes one object to the other, who has to draw it or guess its name, or one child has an object and the other has to work out what it is through asking questions.

Similarities and differences

☛ Make comparisons between now and then and then and then.

☛ Record in Venn diagram or by close observation, make a sketch of the part that is similar or different.

Learning from artefacts

One approach to using artefacts is to follow the line of questioning from *A Teachers' Guide to Learning from Objects* by Durbin, Morris and Wilkinson (English Heritage). An adapted version of their list is given below.

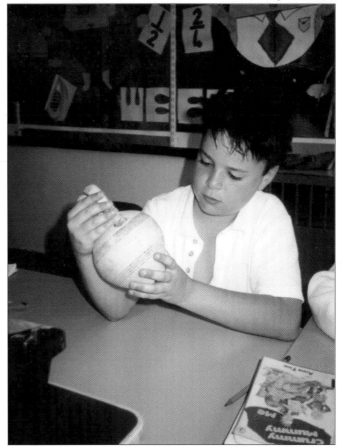

What does it feel like and look like?	What is it made from? What colour is it? What does it smell like? Is the object complete? Has it been altered, adapted, mended in any way? Are there signs of wear?
How was it made?	Was it made by hand or machine? Was it made in a mould or in pieces? How has it been fixed together? Can you see where it is fixed together?
What was it made for?	How has the object been used? Has the use changed? Who would have used it? Can you still use it?

Is it well designed?	Does it do the job it was meant for well? Were the best materials used? Is it decorated? How is it decorated? Do you like the way it looks? Would other people like it?
What is it worth? Who would have owned it?	Is it worth a lot of money? Is it very rare? Is it of great sentimental value to someone? Who owned it originally? Who owns it now?
What do you know of its history?	What has happened to it between the time it was made and today? Who can we ask to tell us more about it?

Learning from photographs

Using photographs to find out about the past is a requirement of Key Element 4 – Historical Enquiry in both key stages. Photographs are relatively easy sources to acquire and most schools should be able to build up a range of examples from the latter half of the nineteenth century through to the present day, depicting many aspects from both programmes of study.

A mother and children making brushes in the 1890's

Types of photographs

☞ All photographs should be in focus and both colour and black and white should be used. Modern black and white photos as well as colour ones should be available.

☞ Photographs should include ones of:
  ● the children
  ● other people of different ages
  ● everyday life, work, leisure and culture
  ● reconstructions in museums
  ● buildings and sites
  ● the school at different times in the past
  ● the local area at different times in the past.

☞ Where possible, photographs should reflect the social, cultural, religious and ethnic diversity of societies studied.

Activities with photographs

The children could follow a particular line of enquiry as demonstrated by the questions opposite or carry out one of the activities below:

Speech bubbles

☞ Children add their own speech bubbles to particular characters in the photograph. They decide what they might be saying in the historical context of the photograph.

Sequencing photos

☞ The children sequence photos of themselves or other people or photos that clearly demonstrate change in everyday life – cars, houses or costume.

Collection of evidence

☞ Use a collection of photos to stimulate writing about an aspect of life or an event, such as Victorian schools. Use other forms of evidence to build on original description.

Portraits

☞ Compare a photograph with a portrait of a place or a person. Which is more realistic and why?

Learning from photographs

A contemporary photograph of Victorian street-urchins.

What do you think the photograph is about?	Is it about a person or a group of people? Is it about a special event or an everyday event?
Why was the photograph taken?	Who do you think took the photograph? Did they decide to take it or were they asked to by someone else? Why did they want to record that particular scene? Who was meant to see the photograph?
Where do you think the photograph was taken?	Was the photograph taken inside or outside? If inside, what sort of building was it taken in? Was it taken in a photographer's studio or elsewhere? Is it posed or a snapshot?
When do you think the photograph was taken?	Are there any clues that tell us when it was taken? Is there anything else in the photograph that will help us to date it, eg background, clothes, buildings, transport?
What can the photograph tell us about life at the time?	How useful is the photograph in telling us about other aspects at this time? How typical are the events/people in the photograph? What other information would be useful to tell us about life at the time?
What doesn't the photograph tell us about life at the time?	Has all the photograph survived? What else might have been happening that the photographer did not capture on film? Do you think the photographer selected a particular image to convey a message?
What is similar or different from life today?	Choose a particular aspect to compare in more detail: • technology • transport • children/adults • work/leisure • style of the photograph.

Learning from portraits

Portraits can be used at Key Stage 1 to help children find out about famous men and women in the past. At Key Stage 2, they can be used for any study unit based after the early sixteenth century.

Slides or postcard copies of many portraits are easily available. However, children should see the real thing when at all possible and know about the size of the original.

Portraits were usually commissioned by rich, important people to celebrate and show off their wealth and status, or to commemorate an event. They are therefore only of limited use when we want to find out about everyday life or other aspects of the time when it was painted.

Children will need to be encouraged to observe the portraits closely. They will also need help with decoding some of the messages and symbols to be found in the paintings.

Activities with portraits

Pouncing

☛ Make your own copy of a portrait using the method the original artist would have used (called pouncing). Make pin prick marks around the outline of someone on a copy of a portrait. Rub charcoal or chalk through the holes on to paper underneath (this is called pouncing). Complete the outline, add details and paint your portrait.

Speech bubbles

☛ Draw speech bubbles and add statements that the sitter is making about themselves in the portrait. For example, "I am the Queen, I am very rich and powerful. I am also very strong and clever. You would be advised not to argue or disagree with me!"

Making miniatures

☛ Make miniatures of yourself, friends and family in the style of old ones.
☛ Sequence your miniatures on a time-line.
☛ Place your miniatures on a family tree.

Different messages

☛ Design and paint a copy of a portrait that gives a different message from the one intended by the original, for example Henry VIII as a rather small, insignificant, weak ruler. What symbols, clothes and setting will you use to display this? What facial expression will he have?

Learning from portraits

The main and supplementary questions below are a useful line of enquiry for children focusing on Key Element 4 – Historical enquiry.

Mr and Mrs George Byam and their eldest daughter, Selina, by Thomas Gainsborough (Bridgeman Art Library).

Who is represented in this picture?	Is there just one sitter or is it a group portrait? Is it male or female, a child or an adult? What is the sitter's name? Who were they?	**How was the picture made?**	What is the artist's name and when did he or she live? What medium has the artist used? What size is the portrait? Does the frame show any special details? Where was the portrait hung originally?
What is the picture trying to tell us? **How does it convey this message?**	Describe the sitter's clothes, facial expression, pose or gesture. Is the portrait flattering or realistic? What does the artist want us to think about the sitter?	**Is there any evidence of where and why it was made?**	Describe the background or setting of the portrait. Was it painted to record an important event? What sort of people would have seen the painting when it was first made? Who can see it today?
Is there any other type of evidence that might tell us more about the picture?	Could we find out more from: ● other portraits? ● photographs? ● documents?		

Learning from buildings and sites

The local environment is an excellent starting point for work involving buildings and sites. It shows children that history is all around them and not just in books or in museums. Fieldwork gives them the opportunity to realise that their locality was built up over a long period of time and they may be able to observe examples of gradual or more dramatic change.

All types of buildings and sites should be studied, from the everyday types, such as houses, schools, churches, shops, railway stations, cinemas, factories, garages and bridges, to the grander palaces and castles.

Buildings and sites provide evidence about the people who designed, built, used or changed them. A study of some of these people will help to bring these large forms of evidence to life.

Maps, plans and aerial photographs will help the children to understand the extent of a building or site.

A 16th-century almshouse.

Activities with buildings and sites

Information guides

- ☞ Make a tape recording describing the place for a blind person.
- ☞ Take photographs of the place and make a trail for younger children to follow.
- ☞ Write estate agents' details describing the building when it was first built.

Own interpretations

- ☞ Look closely at the remains of the building or site. Consider any other evidence related to it and then draw your own interpretation of the place when it was originally built.

Stratigraphy

- ☞ Children work in small groups. One group recreates an archaeological site by burying coins and pottery (reproductions) related to particular periods in the past. Another group has to dig up the finds, identify and record the evidence.

Museum shop

- ☞ Design a museum shop and its contents related to a particular building or site.
  - What would it contain?
  - Why have you chosen these particular items?
- ☞ Design a poster to advertise your building or site.

- ☞ Other sources of information about a local building or site could be obtained from:

  - reference library
  - local museum
  - local history society
  - regional archivist
  - regional archaeological service.

ℒearning from buildings and sites

These suggestions for main and supplementary questions are adapted from *Teaching History at Key Stage 1* NCC INSET resources (1993).

Inner-city terraced housing for working-class people in the 19th century.

What is this place?	Was it a home? A house, castle or palace? Was it used for a particular purpose? School, workhouse or air-raid shelter? When was it built? Who used it or lived in it?
Why might it have been built here?	Was it because of: –the availability of building materials? –a good water supply? –defence reasons?
Why do you think it was built this size?	Was it built to impress others? Was it built to accommodate the number of people who used it or lived in it? Did the cost of building materials influence the size?
Why might it have been built this shape?	Was the shape fashionable at the time it was built? Were they always built this shape? Is the shape important to the function of the building?

The remains of Dunluce Castle, Northern Ireland.

Why do you think it has this layout?	Is it connected to the number and status of the people who lived in or used the building?
Why do you think it looks like this?	Why were these building materials selected? Why is it this height? Why is it decorated in this way? Who designed and built it?
What is it used for now?	Is it used for the same purpose? Has the use of the building changed? Once or many times? What might it be used for in the future?

A PRIMARY TEACHER'S HANDBOOK – *History*

ℒearning from written evidence

Children from both key stages are able to find out about the past from written sources. Anything that includes text, no matter how small, is a written source, from simple advertisements and bus tickets to more detailed documents, such as census returns and newspaper reports.

The key to successful work with written sources is to differentiate either the task or the material used to make the text accessible to all individuals.

One way to do this with young children is to use text combined with an artefact, for example packaging, as this should stimulate them to investigate the words as well as the object.

As children study more time periods in the past, they should begin to realise that the further back you go in time, the less documentary evidence is available to read and study.

Ancient Egyptian hieroglyphics.

𝒲ritten sources to use

The list of written sources is endless, but here are some suggestions of ones more readily available:

- ☞ everyday sources – adverts, bus tickets, labels, packaging
- ☞ linked to a locality – maps, trade directories, census returns, locality inventories, estate agents' details
- ☞ linked to communication or the media – newspapers, comics, plays, cartoons, magazines, TV and radio schedules
- ☞ personal sources – diaries, letters, autobiographies
- ☞ linked to a particular institution – log books, text books, inspectors' reports related to a particular school.

𝒜ctivities from written evidence

True or false

- ☞ Give the children a series of true or false statements about the document. After they have read the document they have to say which pieces of information are contained in the source.

Own documents

- ☞ After reading and researching selected documents, the children produce their own copies. This works well with copies of school reports, newspapers and diaries.

Interpretations

- ☞ Read an eye witness account of a famous person or event. Ask the children to draw their own interpretation. Compare with other children's.

Explaining documents

- ☞ This activity is useful for older children. Ask them to think of ways to explain a document and make it easier for younger children. They could type it out if the writing is difficult to read, dramatise its contents, write an abridged version or explain it verbally.

A PRIMARY TEACHER'S HANDBOOK – *History*

Learning from written evidence

What do you think it is?	Is it a: – diary? – eye witness account? – letter? – newspaper article? – report? – map?
Who might have written it?	Was it written by a child or an adult; a man or a woman? When did they write it? Is it contemporary to the recorded events?
Why was it written?	What does it record? Why did someone at the time want it recorded? Why has it survived?
Is it personal and private or official and public?	Is it written by hand or is it printed? Were we meant to have read it, or was it a secret?

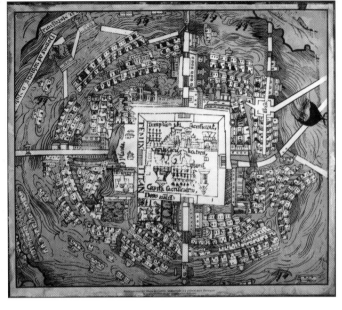

A Spanish plan of Mexico City (formerly the Aztec capital Tenochtitlan) from the 16th century.

What information does it give us?	Does it give information about: – people? – events? – lifestyle: leisure, holidays, work? – places? – ideas?
Is the document reliable as evidence?	Can you detect a particular point of view in the document? Are you suspicious about anything in the document? Why?
What information doesn't it give us?	Does the document leave out important information? Is all of the document available to read?
What other evidence might be useful?	Could we find out more from: – other documents? – other forms of evidence: artefacts, pictures, photographs? – other people's views about the document?

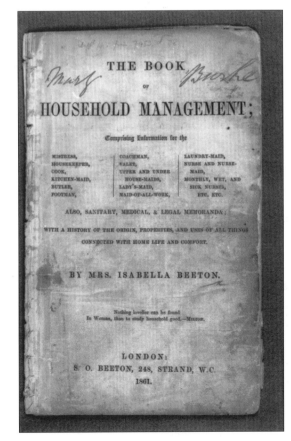

Learning from people

Finding out about the past from adults talking about their past is a requirement of the Key Stage 1 Programme of Study. At Key Stage 2, it is good practice to use oral history for the study units on local history and Britain since 1930.

Oral history is a form of evidence that relies on memory. It can take the form of someone talking to the class in person, a pre-recorded tape or film of someone's reminiscences or the transcript of a talk.

Why use oral history?

- ☞ It can bring history to life and make children realise that the subject is about real people.
- ☞ It gives children access to people whose past is not usually recorded in official documents.
- ☞ It allows the children to develop their own lines of historical enquiry through questioning (Key element 4).
- ☞ It enables children to take part in the actual process of being an historian when they make a record of the past of the adult involved.

People to consider

- ☞ yourself
- ☞ ex-pupils of the school
- ☞ people who work in the school
- ☞ families of the children – parents, grandparents
- ☞ retired workers who can talk about their jobs.

Age Concern and day centres may be able to suggest particular people. A local history society may also help with making contacts.

Topics to consider

- ☞ childhood, schooldays
- ☞ evacuation, rationing
- ☞ holidays, hobbies, leisure activities
- ☞ change in some aspect – clothes, transport

Planning issues

Remember that many people will not be experienced in talking to large groups of young children and will appreciate being briefed beforehand about possible questions. You may need to remind them to try to use appropriate vocabulary for the age and ability of your class.

You will also need to prepare the children for the visit. If the person is not able to travel to the school, you could visit their home, either by yourself or with a small group of children. The whole interview could be taped for the rest of the class.

Learning from people

Some of the following main or supplementary questions should be considered prior to the interview. A very structured, teacher-led approach will be necessary for younger children. However, by the second half of Key Stage 2, the main questions could be posed to small groups of children to allow them to plan their own enquiry.

Who will we ask to talk to us about their past?	Will it be a parent or grandparent? Will it be someone who has a connection with our school? Will it be someone who has a special story to tell? How old are they? When were they born? How will we contact them?
What do we want to find out?	What particular aspect of their life will we ask them to focus on? Is there a specific event that they could describe to us? Can we make a list of questions that we can ask during the interview?
What do we need to tell the person before their visit?	Will it help if we give them some information about us? Would they like to know our questions beforehand? Will we ask them to bring in some things such as old photographs or objects to help us learn about the past?
What will happen during the interview?	Will the person come to our school or will we meet them in a different place? Will we ask our visitor to talk to all the class or small groups? Who will ask the questions?

How will we record the interview?	Will we tape the interview? Can we make a video film of the visit? Will we take some photographs? Will we record the visit in writing or by drawings?
What will happen after the visit?	If we present our work in a display or class assembly shall we invite the visitor to see this? Shall we send them copies of the photographs and our work? How will we thank the person? How will we decide if we have found out what we wanted to know?
What other information would be useful for our enquiries?	Shall we ask someone else to come in so that we can compare their experiences? Would we find other evidence, like photographs and documents, useful?

Learning from stories

The value of appropriate stories in the teaching and learning of history cannot be underestimated. OFSTED considered it important enough to quote from the HMI document *History from 5 to 16* – 'There is an important and central place in history for "good stories, well told ..."', when describing what constitutes good teaching in the original *Handbook for Inspection of Schools*.

Stories should be selected that will help children to achieve learning objectives from the history Programme of Study. However, there are some books which can be used to develop a particular idea, such as different viewpoints, even though those books are not historical in content. This is particularly appropriate in Key Stage 1 where a familiar story could be used before discussing the idea in a historical context.

A good example is *The Three Little Pigs*. Different versions can be found in:

Three Little Pigs (Ladybird Books).
The True Story of the Three Little Pigs Jon Scieszka (Puffin Books).
The Three Little Wolves and the Big Bad Pig Eugene Trivizas (Mammoth).

Which stories should you use?

☞ Children should be told or read a range of different stories. They might include the following:
  – myths, legends
  – eye-witness accounts
  – diaries
  – autobiographies, biographies
  – plays, musicals
  – fiction
  – factual narratives
  – picture story books
  – oral history.
☞ Stories are also available in the form of films and TV programmes.

A human body preserved in a peat bog.

Activities with stories

Stories provide children with a window to another time and place. Their curiosity can be built on with some of the following suggestions:
☞ Sequence events in a story from the past.
☞ Rewrite part of a story from the viewpoint of one of the characters.
☞ Role-play a story, writing a script for one of the characters.
☞ Write a story that tells the history of your life.
☞ Draw pictures to represent different parts of the story. Record in concertina format.
☞ Use a collection of artefacts as a stimulus for creative writing.

A PRIMARY TEACHER'S HANDBOOK – *History*

Learning from stories

What is the story called?	Does the story have a name? Do we all know it by the same name? Do we know who wrote the story originally? Has it been changed in any way? Has it been told and never written down?
What form of story is it?	Is it fiction or a true story? Is it an eye-witness account? Is it the story of someone's life? Was it a secret story, or were we meant to have read it? Is it a long or short story?
What is it about?	When is it set? Where is it set? Who is in it?
What happens in the story?	Can you identify the main events of the story? Can you sequence the main events of the story?

A 19th-century toy horse.

Why does this happen?	Can you give a reason for some or all the events you have mentioned above? Remember to base your answers on your knowledge of the story and that time in history.
Do you know the story? Is this the same version as the one you know?	Why do you think the story was written in this way? What other versions do you know? How does your version differ from the one told today?
What does the story tell us about life at that time?	What other information does the story give us? Is it accurate? How typical are the people and events in the story? What other information would be useful to tell us about life at the time?

A 19th-century baby-walker.

Historical investigations

Finding out about the past or collecting and using evidence can be compared to fitting together the pieces of a jigsaw or the work of a detective.

Children can become historical detectives by taking part in some of these activities that help to develop Key Element 4 – Historical enquiry.

Using broken pottery

This is a useful activity to try before any work related to archaeology, such as in the past non-European society study unit.

☞ Collect some pieces of broken pottery or break up an old cup or saucer. Try to collect some plain, some patterned pieces, a variety of different materials and things used for different purposes. Ask the children what they think it is. What was it when it was complete? What did it look like and what was it used for? Can they draw a picture of their interpretation of the complete object?

Learning objectives
To understand how archaeology is used in finding out about the past and to realise that there are many different interpretations of the past.

Using personal evidence

This idea is useful for children at any time, but especially before using artefacts or other sources related to individuals. There are many variations on it. Here are four tried-and-tested ones:

1 Collect in a bag evidence of you and your life. Ask the children to whom they think it belongs. What does the evidence tell us about the person?

2 Ask children to bring in evidence about themselves – five to ten things that belong to them and would be good clues about their identity. Can the rest of the class guess the owner of the evidence?

3 Collect evidence belonging to different adults in the school. Can the children discover which bag belongs to which adult?

4 Make up an historical evidence bag, say, for a child who was evacuated. It could contain a ration book, coins, name tag, gas mask. The children have to guess who might have owned it and what happened to them.

Learning objectives
To consider the usefulness of evidence, to realise there may be a deficiency of evidence and to ask and answer questions.

Using class or school evidence

This is a good activity to try out before work on artefacts or a museum visit.

☞ Make a museum for the future about your class or school. Collect the evidence, draw the museum pieces or write labels to describe them. Have we all selected the same things? Will we be giving different messages about life today to people in the future?

Learning objectives
The same as for Using personal evidence, but also to develop awareness of different interpretations.

Recreating a Victorian classroom.

𝒰sing photographs (i)

This is a useful Key Stage 1 activity for work on everyday home life in the past.

☛ Start with a photograph of a modern room or house from a magazine. Ask questions such as: Who lives here? How many adults/children? Are there any pets? What do the people like to eat? What other things do they do? The children could also work in pairs asking each other questions about a picture. Then use similar questions for a picture of a room or house from the time period being studied. (You could use a museum reconstruction room on a postcard for this.)

Learning objectives
To find out about the past from photographs and to ask and answer questions about the past.

𝒰sing photographs (ii)

This is a good task to try before any work on portraits and when you want to discuss the power of particular images with children.

☛ Use a Polaroid camera and let the children take some photographs of themselves with the intention of projecting a certain image. Can they look stern, weak, rich, clever, powerful? What expressions do they make to project this image? What clothes could they wear? How should they pose? You can then use postcard portraits of famous people in the past to discuss the image projected by their portrait.

Learning objectives
To find out about the past from pictures and photographs and to ask and answer questions about the past.

Differentiation

Differentiation is described by OFSTED as 'the matching of work to the different capabilities of individuals or groups of pupils in order to extend their learning' (*The Handbook for the Inspection of Schools*).

In reality, differentiation means letting every child get started, letting every child achieve and removing any barriers to participation.

It does not mean planning and teaching individualised programmes of work, except for a few exceptional children at either end of the spectrum.

We also need to be reminded of '...the idea that at any one time learning tasks in nine subjects can be exactly matched to the needs and abilities of all the pupils in a class is hopelessly unrealistic. Match and differentiation are critical to effective learning, but they are aspirations rather than absolutes.' (*Curriculum Organisation and Classroom Practice in Primary Schools* DES 1992.)

Children bring many different levels of experience and understanding of history to the classroom. Differentiated activities should build on these differences and past achievements by presenting appropriate challenges alongside high yet realistic expectations.

Once you have planned an appropriate strategy for differentiation, you also need to consider an appropriate form of classroom organisation, teaching style and resources.

A very simple form of evaluation at the end of the lesson is to ask:
– Were all the children able to start their planned activity?
– Did all the children make progress in the lesson?

Approaches to differentiation

☛ There are four main strategies for differentiation:

By task:
– different tasks given to different groups or individuals;
– stepped tasks where each task is progressively harder;
– a main common task but with modifications and extensions for some children.

By outcome:
– same task to all children, but one that allows a variety of responses at different levels.

By support:
– teacher input and support
– specialist learning support
– other children acting as response partners
– use of technology.

By resources:
– variety of resources available: objects, pictorial and written evidence
– accessibility of all written materials.

☛ Some of these strategies may be more suitable for history than others. Some teachers may feel more confident with some strategies than others. The criteria for choice should be fitness for purpose.

Differentiation across key stages

The revised order allows more flexibility for using material from other key stages than that which the majority of children are studying. The material should be presented in contexts suitable to the child's age. With children who are in this category, the most appropriate approach would be to use material from the key elements from a different key stage rather than the content from the areas of study or study units. This would allow an in-depth and enriched study of a particular topic and not risk the repetition of aspects of the content.

A PRIMARY TEACHER'S HANDBOOK – *History*

Differentiation using a research matrix

☛ Research matrices are a useful way of targeting tasks for particular children or the whole class. Groups could work on one matrix (about display-board size) in the classroom. Provide a series of questions along the top axis which get progressively harder towards the right. The vertical axis should contain different sources, again getting progressively harder. The purpose of this is to give particular children a question to answer relating to one of the sources. All children can contribute to the matrix but with work targeted at their own level of ability.

☛ Matrices could be devised for simple written responses and drawings. Another example is given below. The learning objective for this activity for Key Stage 1 would be to learn about everyday life of children in the past beyond living memory using a range of sources of information.

Differentiation using film or television

☛ Films and television programmes are often under-used, but many are useful in history lessons. They are a form of interpretation which should be used to develop Key element 3. Differentiated responses to the same input can be expected from the children. This will make greater use of the resource and demand more than passive acceptance of the film and its message from the children.

☛ An example is given here of how differentiated activities could be planned around a short extract from the video *Oliver!* when watched in connection with Study Unit 3a: Victorian Britain. The learning objective for this activity would be to learn about the lives of people at different levels of society in town and country at work.

☛ Show the children the first ten minutes of the film (workhouse scene). Ask different groups of children, depending on ability, to watch for information about children's food, adults' food, children's clothes, adults' clothes, buildings and furniture, the roles of men and women and feelings and atmosphere.

☛ Each group discusses their ideas and presents information to the rest of the class. Each group could also ask the rest of the class a question about their presentation to check how much they have understood.

☛ Alternatively, ask each group to discuss their ideas after the video and then split up and re-group with a member of each of the other groups. Each group member then tells the rest of the group about their aspect of the film. This ensures that every member of the original group understands their aspect and is prepared to talk to their new group about it. No-one is allowed to opt out.

Sample research matrix

Sources \ Questions	What toys did Victorian children play with?	Are Victorian toys similar or different to our toys today?	Can you think who would have played with these toys?
Postcard showing Victorian toys from a museum.			
Description of toys from a modern history book.			
Contemporary accounts of Victorian toyshop or penny bazaar.			

Questions to challenge

Questioning is a fundamental part of teaching. In history there are certain questions that should underpin all aspects of work.

- How do we know?
- What do I know for sure?
- What else would I like to know?
- How can I find out more?

Questions related to the key elements should also be asked as part of teaching and day-to-day assessment. Part of Key element 4 requires children to ask and answer questions about the past. Ways to ensure they ask questions include:

- At the beginning of a topic, ask the children to write down ten questions they want to answer during their study.
- Let them take it in turns to be responsible for the class museum or display. As part of their role they have to make labels with questions for the rest of the class to answer.
- Have a weekly question-and-answer session about the topic. All the class have to think of questions that could be included. Select 20 from their suggestions.
- Some children research a famous person in history and become that person for five minutes. The rest of the class can ask the person questions.
- All the class are given the name of a different person in history to stick on their backs. The name is secret from them and they can only find out who it is by asking the others questions.

Effective questioning

An awareness and consideration of some of the following points should lead to more effective questioning:

- ☞ Ensure a balance between open and closed questions. Closed questions are useful to test factual recall but may not allow children to demonstrate understanding.
- ☞ Match the question to the children's level of understanding.
- ☞ Give enough time for responses.
- ☞ Don't ask too many questions at once.
- ☞ Value and build on answers.
- ☞ Don't ask only those children who will know the answers.
- ☞ Don't ask a question and then answer it yourself.
- ☞ Allow for more than one possible answer.
- ☞ Involve all children in the lesson.
- ☞ Ensure your input is of a high level. Speculate and hypothesise to stimulate more discussion and further questioning.

Questions about a society

When learning about everyday life in a society in the past, there will be particular lines of enquiry that the children will need to follow.

- ☞ When did these people live?
- ☞ What were their homes like?
- ☞ What was their diet like?
- ☞ What were their clothes like?
- ☞ What technology was available to them?
- ☞ What were their beliefs?
- ☞ How was life different for men, women and children?
- ☞ How were they employed?
- ☞ How did they enjoy themselves?
- ☞ What was life like for the different social classes?
- ☞ How were they educated?
- ☞ What is the same or different about them and us?
- ☞ What is the same or different about them and another society that we have studied?
- ☞ What is the legacy of their society?

Key questions

The non-statutory guidance of the original history order (1991) recommended key questions or issues as the starting point for each aspect of the plan for a topic or study unit. Examples of key questions are given on pages 16 and 20. Children could be told or given a list of key questions which will help them to structure their recorded work. Some teachers use their key questions as large display headings for different aspects of the work. Telling the children that history is planned this way helps to reinforce the enquiry and research element and show that we won't ever know all the answers.

Asking questions linked to the key elements

1	**Chronology**	When did this happen? How long did it take? What came first, next or last? How does it relate to other events or developments studied? Did this happen before or after the event? What do we call this time in history? In what century did this happen? In what decade did this happen? Which day, month, year comes first?
2	**Range and depth of historical knowledge and understanding**	How was it different from ...? Was it the same as ...? What was it like then? Was it the same everywhere? Did it happen differently in different places? In what ways has this changed? Why did some things change faster than others? Why did this happen? Which reason is the most important? What effect did it have? What were the results?
3	**Interpretation of history**	What are the differences between these two interpretations? Why might there be differences between them? Is this an accurate interpretation? How can we prove it? What other evidence do we need? What would you believe about it if you only had this information? Are there gaps in this story of the past? Which interpretation is more believable?
4	**Historical enquiry**	How do we know? How can we find out? What does this source tell us about the past? Where did it come from? How useful is it? How reliable is it? How can we check a source? Are there gaps in the evidence? Why are we unable to discover what happened from the available evidence?
5	**Organisation and communication**	What can you remember about ...? What can you tell me about ...? What have you learned about ...? Which aspects will you record? How will you structure this information into a record? If you had to describe the meaning of ... to a partner, what would you use and how would you go about it? What different ways could we tell someone about this?

Making recording more exciting

At both key stages, children are required to communicate their knowledge and understanding of history in a variety of ways. This includes structured narratives and descriptions at Key Stage 2.

All children will communicate their knowledge and understanding orally but this and the next page concentrate more on a permanent record.

Providing a structure to their research will support children when they come to write up their findings. The following six questions can be used by all children whenever involved in historical enquiry:

- What do I want to know?

- What do I know about it already?

- What am I going to use for my research?

- What did I find out?

- What more would I like to know?

- How will I answer these new questions?

The children could then evaluate the success of their enquiry:

- Did I find out what I wanted to know?

Children take a break during a trip to an iron-age hill fort.

Make a record of it!

It is tempting for the busy classroom teacher to photocopy some of the countless worksheets from commercial history schemes on the market and ask the class to complete them as a record of their work. While photocopiable sheets have their place there are alternative methods. The following ideas will ensure that the children's topic books don't all look exactly the same!

☞ Write a letter or design a questionnaire for parents and grandparents when researching about everyday life in the past. What do you want to find out? What questions will you ask?
☞ Make labels for a class museum, to go under a time-line or for pictures and photographs. The labels could just include a title or they could also have a description and questions to encourage other children to observe more closely. Write or word-process the labels.
☞ Add your own comments and questions to pictorial evidence. Draw in speech bubbles – what are they saying?
☞ Write questions around the edge which another group have to answer.
☞ Write down the answers to ten questions connected with your history topic. Pass to a partner who has to think of the questions for each answer. At the end, record both questions and answers.

Recording visits

Recording work after a visit to a museum, gallery, building or site can be difficult, if the children have to rely on ticks or short answers to questions on the project worksheets. One approach is to pose a holistic question to the visit instead of the usual worksheet. The following suggestions will give you a starting point for devising a range of such questions.

☛ You are responsible for designing the Tudor range of goods for the museum shop. Make sketches suitable for the range in addition to a logo and carrier bags. What other information do you need?

☛ Design a new range of crockery based on Greek myths. Make sketches and research the necessary details, ready to make a prototype plate back at school.

The children's safety is paramount if historical enquiry involves a trip to an old mine-working.

Extended writing

Opportunities to produce extended writing at Key Stage 2 and for older, more able children at Key Stage 1 should be provided to allow children to structure their descriptions and narratives in a way that will motivate their interest and involvement. Experiment with some of the following ideas:

☛ Reproduce a contemporary document such as a journal, diary, letter, or handbill. What will it look like? How will you make it look old? How will you research the contents?

☛ Write a prospectus or brochure for a school in the past. Give details about the building and the curriculum. Try this for a Victorian school or a homefront school during the Second World War.

☛ Write your own myth or legend in the style of others. Write a story using a scene on a piece of pottery as a stimulus.

☛ Write your own eye-witness account of a famous event in the past. How did you feel? What did you see? Who did you tell about it?

☛ Become a spy and send a secret letter written in code. Make a wax seal so you will know if your message has been intercepted. Send a message from the court of Queen Elizabeth I. Write a script for a radio or TV news programme reporting on a famous event in the past. Who will you interview? Who can provide an eye witness report?

☛ Write newspaper reports or just headlines from different viewpoints. Write in the style of a tabloid or a broadsheet.

☛ Research and then write *A day in the life of ...* a non-famous person from the past. Use evidence about a real person, for example, a Victorian child working down the mines.

Using information technology

The common requirements of the programmes of study state that 'Pupils should be given opportunities, where appropriate, to develop and apply their information technology (IT) capability in their study of history'. IT allows children to organise and communicate historical information and to investigate sources which otherwise would be difficult to manage and organise in the classroom.

IT simulation programs should be used as an alternative form of interpretation.

Other sources of information

Information about history and information technology can be obtained from:

National Council for Educational Technology
Milburn Hill Road
Science Park
Coventry CV4 7JJ
Tel: 01203 416994

SCAA has produced guidance to support the revised Order for IT Key Stages 1 and 2: *Information Technology – the New requirements* (SCAA 1995).

This booklet gives examples of the requirements of the IT Order. Many of them are given in the context of other curriculum areas including history.

Key Stage 1 suggestions for IT activities

- ☞ Use a word processor to write simple stories about famous people and events.
- ☞ Use a word processor to write labels for a class museum or display.
- ☞ Use a time-line program to study own and family history.
- ☞ Use an overlay keyboard to find out information from a map, picture or portrait.
- ☞ Add information to a database obtained from a questionnaire to parents and grandparents.
- ☞ Use a CD-ROM to research and select information relevant to a topic.
- ☞ Use a word processor to produce a class agreed list of questions to put to a visitor talking about their past.
- ☞ Set up a database to record information about items in a class museum. What information needs to be recorded? What is recorded in other museums?

Key Stage 2 suggestions for IT activities

- ☞ Use word processing and desk-top publishing to produce newspaper headlines and stories about past events.
- ☞ Use a time-line program to study developments in local history.
- ☞ Use a simulation program to compare interpretations with evidence.
- ☞ Use databases to investigate and interpret sources containing numerical information.
- ☞ Add information to a time-line for the study unit being studied. Search and sort the time-line database chronologically.
- ☞ Use a CD-ROM to research and select information relevant to a topic.
- ☞ Record information about the local area for future classes to research when investigating change.

Classroom practice

Effective lessons

☞ For a lesson to be effective, certain features should be present. Some of these are:
  – clear learning objectives, shared with the children
  – work matched to ability
  – appropriate organisation for the task
  – good control and classroom management
  – an enthusiastic approach
  – appropriate use of resources
  – pace and good use of time
  – a clear focus of learning.
☞ All of these features should result in some progress in knowledge, skills and understanding for the children.

Valid historical tasks

The features listed above are relevant for all subject areas and all lessons. With classroom practice in history it is important to ensure that the children are carrying out valid historical tasks. The following checklist should help you to ensure this.

What are the learning objectives for the activity?
– Which skills will be developed?
– Which areas of knowledge and understanding will be acquired?
– Which concepts will be learned?

How will children learn?
Which of the following will they use?
– documents and printed sources
– artefacts
– pictures and photographs
– buildings and sites
– interpretations

Which methods of class organisation will you use?
– teacher presentation
– group work
– individual research
– role-play, drama
– class discussion
– class brainstorm

How will they present their work?
– orally
– visually
– in writing
– drama
– IT

Will the children be encouraged to ask and answer questions?

Will the children be encouraged to select and organise historical information?

Is there a balance of activities that allows children to learn about:
– the lives of men, women and children?
– different cultural, social and ethnic groups?

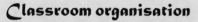

Classroom organisation

There is no one right way to organise a class. At different times whole-class teaching, group work or individual learning will be appropriate. The main criterion for choice must be fitness for purpose.

How you organise your class will be determined by:

– the learning objectives for the activity
– the children's needs, educational and social
– the teacher's needs and level of adult support available
– the nature of the activities
– space and resources available.

Deciding on the best approach

☛ Use this table to help you decide on the best approach to classroom organisation. Look at the different forms of organisation listed in the left hand column. If they allow for the opportunities listed along the top, then place a tick or a comment in the box. Your findings from this could be discussed with colleagues and could form the basis of advice about appropriate organisational strategies as part of your school's history policy.

	Opportunities for using evidence and interpretations	Opportunities for discussion and debate	Opportunities for role-play and drama	Opportunities for question and answer
Teacher presentation				
One or two groups on history activities as part of group rotation with activities from other curriculum areas				
Circus of activities				
Group work on identical tasks				
Group work on different tasks				
Individual work on identical tasks				

Successful group work

☛ If your class is not used to working in a group there are certain things you can do to make the activity more successful. Make sure that:
– the objective for the task is very clear
– the activity is relatively short and focused – think of six questions about your artefact that the next group can try to answer
– the group have their own rules to keep to: all listen to each other, all take it in turns
– everyone in the group has a turn to be group leader, reporter, presenter.

A PRIMARY TEACHER'S HANDBOOK – *History*

Classroom organisation

One way to ensure effective practice is to monitor or evaluate existing practice with the purpose of considering ways to develop and improve it. Everyone in the school can be involved in this process, but for the purpose of this handbook the focus is on the roles of the class teacher, history co-ordinator and the children. Any system of evaluation or monitoring should be based on shared aims and values.

The starting point, therefore, for the teachers involved must be a discussion and consideration of what are valid historical tasks. (See page 57 for a checklist.)

Monitor and improve

☛ **What can class teachers do?**
  – reflect on own practice
  – talk to the children
  – check outcomes (children's work) against intended learning objectives (in plans).

☛ **What can the history co-ordinator do?**
  – evaluate plans
  – observe classroom practice
  – sample children's recorded work throughout the school
  – interview and talk to colleagues.

☛ **What can the children do?**
  – evaluate their own work at the end of a topic or study unit
  – consider ways to improve their work.

The children

Children's contribution to evaluation and monitoring of practice is often marginalised, if not completely ignored in many schools. Their comments and judgements on aspects of the teaching of history should be considered as part of a balanced range of evidence. If asked often enough, children will give honest, useful answers. Involving them in evaluation sends out a clear message that their opinion is valued. It is also vital if they are to begin to understand what a good piece of history work looks like, as opposed to a neat piece of work. The process also supports them in the task of deciding which particular pieces of work need improving and the strategies for going about it.

Evaluation questions
☛ Which is your best piece of history work? Why?
☛ Which is your worst piece of history work? Why?
☛ What was the most surprising thing you discovered in this topic?
☛ What else would you like to know about this topic?
☛ What did you use to find out about this topic?
☛ Did you work better on your own, in a pair, in a group or with the whole class?
☛ Which activity helped you to learn the most? Why?
☛ If this topic is taught to another class next year, what would you like to change for them?

Improving their own work
☛ To improve their work, children need to have success criteria explained to them. This means saying something along the lines of: 'A good piece of history work will tell me why something happened and what happened as a result of it. It won't be copied from a book but will be your own writing after you have read the documents and discussed them in your group.'
☛ They can then improve their work by:
  – selecting good/poor pieces of work
  – listing or talking about what makes them good or poor
  – discussing ways to improve
  – setting their own improvement targets for their next history topic
  – checking to see if targets were met
  – deciding if the work is getting better.

Class organisation

Class teachers

Class teachers have a responsibility to provide all children in their class with the best possible educational experiences. Some form of ongoing evaluation or reflection on their own practice is vital to ensure that this is happening.

Self-reflection

☞ A commitment to self-reflection is an important part of being a professional teacher. Focus on an area of your practice that can be reflected upon in the context of your own classroom.

☞ Possible areas include:
  – the existing grouping arrangements for history tasks
  – the accessibility of written evidence for all children
  – reinforcement of the main focus of learning at the end of a session
  – effective use of radio and TV.

☞ Consider any improvements that could be made to your teaching which will lead to greater progress on the part of the children.

Talking to children

☞ Many of the evaluation questions for children (see previous page) are suitable, along with:
  – Did you enjoy doing this work?
  – What have you learned from it?
  – Were you pleased with your work?
  – Was it easy/difficult?
  – Could you explain this to me?
  – What did you use to find out about ...?
  – Would you have liked to have lived then? Why?
  – Are there any characters from that time you would like/not like to be? Why?

☞ The answers to these questions should be useful when deciding how effective the teaching of a particular topic has been.

Check outcomes against objectives

☞ Evaluate plans by highlighting or marking areas of work covered or not covered.
☞ Mark the work of individual children to assess whether learning objectives have been realised by the majority.
☞ Adapt plans to suit time available, resources, children and the National Curriculum, if learning objectives are not being realised.

The history co-ordinator

The role of the co-ordinator is central to curriculum and teaching development. Expectations and perceptions of this role have changed in recent years away from that of someone who supports and provides resources to a manager who has an impact on standards within a subject area. Evaluation and monitoring are therefore vital tools if a co-ordinator is to secure and improve standards.

Talking to colleagues

Talking to colleagues about their practice should open up the possibility of monitoring in a supportive way and offering advice when necessary.

☞ Lines of questioning could include:
  – How did that piece of work develop or happen?
  – What resources did you find useful and what else do you need?
  – Did all the children do the same work and use the same resources?
  – Did you come across any areas of difficulty for yourself or the children?
  – Would you do it the same way a second time around?
  – Did the work fit into the time planned?

The facing page gives further suggestions for the co-ordinator.

Class organisation

Sampling children's recorded work
☛ All work produced for a particular topic (not individual pieces) should be considered for this exercise.
☛ Co-ordinators should also select work from children who are of average, above and below average ability from each class. A particular focus should be selected, outcomes recorded and recommendations made.
☛ Possible lines of enquiry include the following (only one or two should be selected at a time):
   – How is the work marked? Are there useful historical comments?
   – Is there evidence of historical enquiry or research?
   – Are the activities valid historical tasks?
   – Is the work recorded in a variety of forms?
   – Do the activities follow the plans for the topic/unit?
   – Is there evidence of identified key elements and content being taught?
   – Is there evidence of progression throughout each child's work?
   – Is there evidence of different forms of differentiation?
   – Is there evidence of IT where appropriate?
   – Is there evidence of progression throughout the school?

Evaluating plans
☛ Co-ordinators should have the opportunity to evaluate plans written to demonstrate how the learning objectives from the Programme of Study will be taught. Depending on the school, this detail may be given in medium-term plans for the topic or unit, or short-term daily or weekly plans.
☛ Questions to consider include:
   – Does the planning satisfy National Curriculum requirements?
   – Does the planning refer to learning objectives, activities, organisation and differentiation?
   – Are assessment opportunities identified?
   – Is outline or depth of subject matter clear?
   – Are children offered a variety of learning experiences?
   – Is the finished work expected from each child outlined?
   – Is the main focus for each lesson identified?
   – Will the plans fit into the time available?
   – Could a teacher new to the school use the plans?

Observing classroom practice
This form of monitoring gives a co-ordinator a chance to observe what is happening in the classrooms and see whether practice matches the plans. Many staff feel threatened when observed and there is always the possibility of a co-ordinator observing a one-off show lesson. However, if good practice can be identified and disseminated, it gives colleagues an opportunity to draw on each other's experiences and offers a way forward to support weaker areas. Agreed guidelines for classroom observation visits are essential and should include some of the following:

Before the visit
☛ Discuss and agree whole school focus for visits.
☛ Agree time and date of visits to classrooms.
☛ Clarify role of observer.
☛ Arrange time for feedback and possible follow-up visit.
☛ Pre-visit support needed?
☛ Agree how notes taken.

During the visit
☛ Everything agreed to before the visit to be observed.
☛ Thank teacher and children (if possible).
☛ Try to give some immediate positive comment before feedback.

After the visit
☛ Feedback to be given at arranged time within 24 hours of visit (same day if possible).
☛ Discuss observations and recommendations.
☛ Set objectives for future practice.
☛ Feedback to be as positive as possible.

Resources

Some classrooms and resource rooms resemble bookshops or warehouses. Many resources, however, are old, inappropriate and never used. If you have not used something since the introduction of the National Curriculum, then apart from keeping one or two examples for sentimental reasons, throw it away.

A re-enactment of an 18th-century military band.

Resources to enrich and extend

☛ Resources should offer opportunities for differentiated work. For the more able child, the resources should be able to enrich and extend their thinking. Some of the following characteristics should be present for this to happen:
  – A wide variety of activities.
  – Opportunities for further research and development.
  – Many open-ended tasks and questions.
  – Encourages use of imagination.
  – Develops empathy and different perspectives.
  – Gives children responsibility for their own learning and target setting.
  – Involves problem-solving and problem-opposing situations.
  – Encourages higher order thinking skills.

Evaluating their own resources

☛ To gain an insight from the group of people who use the resources, ask the children to evaluate their usefulness regularly.
  – Which resources did you enjoy using? Why?
  – Which ones didn't you enjoy using? Why?
  – Which resources helped you to learn the most? Why?
  – Were any of them difficult to use? Why?
  – Which resources do we need more of?
  – Which resources were easy to use by yourself, with a partner or in a small group?
  – What other resources could we use in or outside the classroom for this topic?
☛ Key Stage 1 children could be asked to select a favourite resource and tell the rest of the class about it in circle time. They can award stars or smiley faces to the resources that have helped them to learn the most. This should help to develop early skills in analysis and criticism of a range of sources of information.

Teacher checklist for children's resources

☛ It is useful to consider how effectively the resources are displayed in the classroom.
  – Are all resources available for all children if they need them?
  – Are the resources bright, attractive, and able to motivate the children?
  – Are the resources accurate and up to date?
  – Do they encourage further research and historical enquiry?
  – Do they contain valid historical activities?
  – Are they able to promote both independent and collaborative work?
  – Do they offer opportunities for differentiated activities?
  – Do they meet the requirements of the National Curriculum?
☛ Old history text books are useful for children to make comparisons between then and now for Everyday life in Key Stage 1 and Britain since 1930 in Key Stage 2. The original Order for History may also serve a similar purpose one day!

Getting the most from your resources

All resources should provide good value for money. This means that they should have some impact on the quality of teaching and learning and be directly related to children's progress in history. Ways to maximise their use:

– Use a staff professional development day for all staff to visit a museum, gallery or site to increase subject knowledge and buy resources.
– Include a checklist of items in resource boxes.
– Display all resources at regular intervals to ensure all staff are aware of the full range.
– Have a regular item on the agenda for staff meetings where teachers can mention a resource and activity that was effective.
– Visit another school to observe their resources and storage systems.
– Ask parents to donate or loan artefacts that could be used in a class or school museum.

Contents for a resource box for a topic or study unit

Resources should reflect the social, cultural, religious and ethnic diversity of societies studied. The roles of men, women and children should be represented. Contents could include:

☞ background information for teachers and children
☞ examples of children's work from a previous year
☞ pictorial evidence – posters, postcards, photographs, pictures
☞ artefacts – real or reproduction
☞ written evidence
☞ videos, tapes, slides
☞ oral history tape or suggestion of someone to contact
☞ music tapes
☞ list of places to visit
☞ IT programs
☞ maps
☞ interpretations
☞ fiction books for teachers and children
☞ costumes and props for role-play.

Children's books

New Clothes for Alex M Dickinson (Hippo).

You'll soon Grow into them, Titch P Hutchins (Red Fox).

The Lost Doll J Richardson (Puffin).

My Grandmother's Patchwork Quilt J Bolton (Tango Books).

Lucy and Tom's Day S Hughes (Puffin).

Grandma's Pictures S Hughes in *Alfie and Annie Rose Storybook* (Red Fox).

Granpa J Burningham (Puffin).

Peepo! J and A Ahlberg (Puffin).

Fourteen Rats and a Rat Catcher T Cole (A & C Black).

Starting School J & A Ahlberg (Puffin).

My Great Grandpa M Waddell (Walker Books).

ƒolens teachers' books

A Time to Remember A primary history scheme that includes full-colour text books and photocopiable teachers' resource books.

Ideas Bank series: *Aztecs, Ancient Greece, Ancient Egypt, Britain Since 1930, Anglo-Saxons, The Indus Valley, Tudor Times, Victorian Britain.*

Brainwaves series: *Aztecs, Ancient Greece, Ancient Egypt, Britain Since 1930, Anglo-Saxons, The Indus Valley, Tudor Times, Victorian Britain, Invasion Britain, Romans, Vikings.*

Photopack series: *Ancient Egypt, Ancient Greece, Vikings, Romans, Anglo Saxons, Victorian Toys, Tudor Monarchs, Britain Since 1930, Home front, Greek Myths and Legends.*

Useful addresses

The Historical Association (59a Kennington Park Road, London SE11 4JH. Tel: 0171 735 3901) publishes two journals, **Teaching History** and **Primary History**, and produces guides to support teaching and learning.

Council for British Archaeology (The Education Officer, The King's Manor, York YO1 2EP. Tel: 01904 433925).

The National Trust (Education Manager, 36 Queen Anne's Gate, London SW1H 9AS. Tel: 0171 222 9251) produces **A Guide to Historic Houses, Castles and Gardens** (new edition every year). It includes opening times, admission charges, maps and background information of most monuments and properties open to the public. This includes English Heritage and National Trust properties.

English Heritage Education Service (Keysign House, 429 Oxford Street, London W1R 2HD. Tel: 0171 973 3442/3) produces a range of teacher's guides including **A Teacher's Guide to Using Portraits** Susan Morris, **A Teacher's Guide to Learning from Objects** G Durbin, S Morris, S Wilkinson, **A Teacher's Guide to Using School Buildings** S Purkis.

History in Evidence (Monk Road, Alfreton, Derbyshire DE55 7RL) produces a wide range of reproduction artefacts for many different periods throughout history. Send for a catalogue.